soap

soap

handmade, pure and natural

TATYANA HILL

This edition is published by Aquamarine

Aquamarine is an imprint of Anness Publishing Ltd
Hermes House, 88–89 Blackfriars Road, London SE1 8HA
tel. 020 7401 2077; fax 020 7633 9499
www.aquamarinebooks.com; info@anness.com

© Anness Publishing Ltd 1999, 2003

This edition distributed in the UK by Aurum Press Ltd,
25 Bedford Avenue, London WC1B 3AT;
tel. 020 7637 3225; fax 020 7580 2469

This edition distributed in the USA and Canada by National
Book Network, 4720 Boston Way, Lanham, MD 20706;
tel. 301 459 3366; fax 301 459 1705; www.nbnbooks.com

This edition distributed in Australia by Pan Macmillan
Australia, Level 18, St Martins Tower, 31 Market St,
Sydney, NSW 2000;
tel. 1300 135 113; fax 1300 135 103;
customer.service@macmillan.com.au

This edition distributed in New Zealand by David Bateman
Ltd, 30 Tarndale Grove, Off Bush Road, Albany, Auckland; tel.
(09) 415 7664; fax (09) 415 8892

A CIP catalogue record for this book is available from the
British Library.

Publisher **Joanna Lorenz**
Senior Editor **Caroline Davison**
Editorial Reader **Hayley Kerr**
Photographer and Stylist **Nicki Dowey**
Production Controller **Karina Han**

Previously published as *Handmade Soap*

10 9 8 7 6 5 4 3 2 1

Publisher's note: The weights and volumes given for the ingredients in
this book have been presented to make the soap-making process as
easy as possible. In general, weight is used for all ingredients, including liquid ones like essential oils. However, where the quantity used is
small (thus making it difficult to weigh on domestic scales) or the
amount is a matter of personal preference, the measurements are given
in teaspoons for ease of use.
    The publisher cannot be held responsible for any injuries that occur
when making the soaps featured in this book.

Contents

introduction

It was probably my grandmother who first put the idea of home-made soap into my head. My grandmother always kept me with her, and I grew up on a diet of stories of country life in the early 1900s. In her day, the majority of people made or traded items such as soap. So, making your own necessities – the things we all now buy at the supermarket – did not seem so strange to me. As a child, I was naturally artistic, and rather than painting or drawing, I liked to make things – useful things.

Away from my grandmother's watchful gaze, I secretly used to make my own cosmetic lines with things found in the bathroom and kitchen cupboards: talcum powder, washing-up liquid, cold cream, petroleum jelly, food colourings and flavourings were mixed together in order to make bubble baths, soaps and lip glosses. As I got older, cornmeal face masks, as well as rose and honey infusions, made birthday gifts for amused relatives. These were the first toiletries I ever made, and discovering a gift for creating them paved the way for my later career when I started making them professionally.

Every time I give soap as a gift, the grateful recipient never fails to be intrigued by the idea that I might have made it myself. They are so appreciative that they linger over the soap, fascinated and hungry for information about the ingredients and processes that went into making it. This gives me a wonderful feeling, and I still feel the same child's pride.

left Honey & Oatmeal Soap, with its wholesome, natural ingredients, promotes healthy skin.

Making soap is an addictive and deeply satisfying process. It is so rewarding to create something that is useful as well as beautiful. I discovered soap-making by accident when, running my home-furnishings shop, I needed a product that I could rely on to fit into the style of my company. Needless to say, the soap quickly took over the company – and my imagination.

Soap is an everyday item, yet all soap, and in particular hand-made soap, has a deep allure. Soap represents a mixture of the practical and the romantic. The bath still holds its own elusive charm for us; it is a place of safety and warmth, filled with sensuality and symbolism. The bathroom is the one place where even the most prudish can be indulgent. Natural hand-made soap is more than a safe, pure and gentle cleanser; it is also a warm, luxurious, personal possession that can be tailor-made for you and your loved ones.

right Clove Soap, with its clove essential oil and layer of real clove buds, is spicy and stimulating.

What is Soap?

Soap is a surfactant which means that it helps water to wet things more evenly. Soap molecules have tails which attract dirt and pull it away from the surface that it is on. The soap then suspends the dirt in a lather until it can be washed away. Soap is made by combining an alkaline solution with animal fats or vegetable oils which are acidic. When mixed under the right circumstances, they neutralize to form a new compound, which we call soap. Saponification is the technical term for this reaction.

The History of Soap

Precious and far more difficult to make than it is today, a piece of soap was once a valuable household item. Mentions of soap go back into antiquity as far as 2500 BC, but the most popular story of how soap was discovered is Roman. Some women were washing their clothes in the River Tiber below Mount Sapo. Animals were burned at Sapo as religious sacrifices. As it rained, the water washed away the animal fats from the sacrifices as well as the alkalis from the ashes. When these substances mixed together, a soapy mixture was made that settled on the rocks. While washing their clothes in the river, the women found that they became cleaner after touching the rocks.

Over the centuries, before the emergence of commercial detergent companies, many rural people made their own soap. Traditionally, soap would have been made with collected and clarified meat drippings from the kitchen, combined with an alkaline solution made from water mixed with wood ashes.

The commercial production of soap started in around 1608, but because soap of this type was generally available only to the rich, it was the soap produced in the home or by small cottage establishments that prevailed. Although scientific advancements in the production of alkalis occurred between the late 18th and mid-19th centuries, soap production was still an unrefined process. Home-made soap was difficult to produce, generally crude and usually caustic, so home producers of the mid-19th and early 20th centuries were thrilled at the arrival of large soap companies which made soap an easily obtainable commodity.

1 Pumice Soap 2 Rope Soap 3 Seaweed Soap 4 Goat's Milk & Almond Soap 5 Vanilla Neapolitan Bar

6 Castile Soap 7 Cinnamon & Orange Soap 8 Calendula Soap 9 Clove Soap 10 Cinnamon Seed Soap 11 Soap Ball

12 Bentonite Clay & Tea Tree Oil Soap 13 Cinnamon & Orange Soap 14 Lavender Olive Oil Soap 15 Cinnamon Seed Soap

Commercial Soap

Soap is made commercially in huge vats by a process called the "continuous method", in which ingredients are continuously added to one end and removed from the other. During this process, the emollient glycerine that naturally exists in soap is removed and sold separately for its moisturizing qualities.

Commercial soap is nearly always made from tallow (animal fat) and usually contains a variety of synthetic chemicals. Because of the lack of glycerine as well as the inclusion of poor-quality ingredients and additives, commercial soap can often irritate and dry the skin, or can cause an allergic reaction. Sadly, even many hand-made soap companies use synthetic fragrances, preservatives and colours in their products.

Although some people cannot use soap, I have found that most can use a soap that is free from questionable or synthetic additives. I am convinced that completely pure soap is the best option, as so many people who have had skin problems all their lives tell me how much they have benefited from using my soaps.

As a soap-producer, I am, of course, tempted to use synthetics in my toiletries. Apart from the bright colours and the selection of aromas available, chemical fixatives and preservatives also solve a host of other problems. However, although it is difficult to produce natural cosmetics commercially, it is easy to achieve at home. After all, hand-made soap involves so much care and effort that it's not worth adding ingredients that compromise the integrity of the soap.

left Frankincense & Myrrh Soap is not only luxurious, but it also has skin-healing properties.

right Lavender Olive Oil Soap has a traditional allure and can be used to help you relax and unwind.

soap types & processes

Soap is made by combining an alkaline solution with fats and/or oils. To produce the alkaline solution, sodium hydroxide is mixed with water. Sodium hydroxide can be obtained from most supermarkets. It is commonly used as a drain and floor cleaner and will probably be labelled caustic soda or lye. I prefer to use mineral water in my recipes which, although not essential, adds to the purity of the final product and is cheaper and easier to obtain than distilled water.

Any fat will combine chemically with the sodium hydroxide, but each fat contributes a different quality to the soap. Tallow and lard, which are rendered from animal fats, are the cheapest and most traditional oils used in soap-making. Tallow makes a very hard soap with a good-quality lather and is used more than any other fat in the production of soap.

Many types of oils, including some exotic ones, can be used to make soap. Some oils from vegetable sources are either difficult to obtain or are too costly in large quantities, so I have developed recipes that use more obtainable basic oils. You should be able to purchase all the oils for the basic soap recipes in a large supermarket. If you are interested in using exotic or therapeutic oils in your own recipes, I would advise adding them as supplements just before pouring, or when milling.

For the purposes of hand-made vegetable-based soap, palm oil has very similar characteristics to tallow. It saponifies easily, is inexpensive and produces a very hard soap. Used alone, palm oil can make soap that is drying and too crumbly. However, including some palm oil in a recipe will create an easy-to-make, well-balanced soap that is moisturizing, lathering and just hard enough to be long-lasting. Look for palm oil in Asian food stores or ask a local bakery or oil wholesaler to provide you with some, but bear in mind that you may have to buy a large quantity. Make sure it is white refined oil – unrefined palm oil has a strong orange hue and is not suitable for these soap recipes.

right Castile Soap is a traditional soap that originated in Spain and generally contains a large quantity of, if not only, olive oil.

Coconut oil is another important oil in soap-making. It creates a silky-textured soap that lathers very well in cold or hard water. You should be able to purchase it at a supermarket, an Asian food store or even a chemist (drugstore). Make sure you buy pure coconut oil and not coconut milk or cream. Coconut oils may be liquid or completely solid at room temperature. I find that the solid variety is the best and should be used for the recipes in this book.

Olive oil adds excellent moisturizing qualities and mildness to a soap. Soaps made with olive oil are known as Castile soap, which originated in Spain and the Mediterranean. However, olive oil is difficult to saponify, makes a fairly soft soap and is expensive when used in large quantities. Although extra virgin oil is considered superior for cooking purposes, a lighter oil from later pressings makes a more desirable soap, without the smoky, olive-oil smell that the virgin grade lends. Adding beeswax will speed up the saponification process greatly and, because it has hardening characteristics, it is the perfect addition to a soap made from large quantities of olive oil.

Soybean and sunflower oil will make a similar soap to that made from olive oil and are cheaper

above Cinnamon Seed Soap, with its attractive marbled pattern, has exfoliating properties and can be used to massage the skin.

alternatives. Replacing some of the olive oil in a recipe that calls for a large quantity will prove less costly and will not compromise the moisturizing or healing properties of the finished soap.

The Cold Process

The "cold process" is the method that you will use to make the basic soaps in this book (see the "Basic Soap Base", pages 26–28). It means that the soap is made using only the heat of the chemical reaction between the combined oil and alkaline ingredients. No external heat is used during saponification. (As the recipes call for some oils that are solid at room temperature, you will have to melt them beforehand so they are able to react with the lye solution. This primary application of heat does not stop the soap from being classified as cold process.)

Hand-milled Soap

Any cold-process soap that has cured can be made into several different hand-milled soaps by grating it, remelting it and adding different scents and colours (see the "Hand-milled Soap Base", pages 30–31). The biggest benefit of hand milling is that you can make one large batch of plain, cold process soap, and then make small batches with different scents and colours without having to make a whole batch of each. This is helpful if you are using an expensive essential oil or experimenting with colour. As the soap is already saponified, there are none of the problems associated with a bad batch, and you know that the soap will be chemically successful.

Caustic soda (lye) can diminish the intensity of scent in essential oils as well as the efficacy of supplements, so adding ingredients during milling, after the soap has reacted and cured, can produce better results than the cold process. Milling soap is also a way to save a batch that didn't work out, although you should not always mill a failed batch (see "Problem Solving", pages 32–33).

Reprocessing Soap

You can also grate down soap that turned out badly or was reserved for milling to create new toiletries without heating or adding water (as you do for hand-milled soap). Compress finely grated slivers into different shapes or add a large quantity of solid or liquid nutrients to make liquid soaps, shaving creams and foaming body scrubs.

below Vanilla Neapolitan Bars, with their three different layers, are striking, elegant soaps.

colours, scents & supplements

Colours

In natural soap-making, bright colours are virtually impossible to achieve. The alkaline nature of soap and natural oxidization changes most bio-source colours. Purple cabbage, blue mallow, black-currant, beetroot (beet) and strawberry turn into various shades of green, brown or mid-grey. This can be frustrating, but colouring a natural soap with an artificial dye negates going to the trouble of making a natural product. For a wider natural colour spectrum, experiment with fully dried, powdered vegetable matter; adding liquid extracts is the cause of many unwanted colour changes.

Scents

In order to scent a batch of soap you need to use scented material of a very high concentration: crushed fruit or flowers will not scent. It is necessary to use some type of concentrated fragrance. I use pure essential oils to scent my soaps. Natural essential oils not only scent the soap, but they contribute other beneficial properties such as inducing sleep or stimulating the mind. Also, most essential oils are antibacterial and antifungal, giving obvious benefits.

An essential oil is the part of a plant that gives it its fragrance – when you peel an orange, the scent you can smell is that of the essential oils being released. Some plants, like mint, and plant parts, such as orange peel, yield a relatively high content of essential oil and are therefore fairly affordable. This is why mint and orange essential oils are widely used in the food and cosmetic industries for scenting and flavouring.

Unfortunately, other plants, such as neroli (orange flower) and rose, contain very little oil, are extremely costly and are therefore rarely used in commercially available products. As chemical copies are cheaper, the scents of pure extracts and natural essential oils are often adulterated or even completely synthesized in

opposite · Natural Colours: **1** Plain (semi-sweet) chocolate **2** Ground coffee **3** Cinnamon **4** Cocoa powder **5** Powdered instant tea **6** Mint **7** Turmeric **8** Paprika **9** Mixed herbs

commercial products. Synthetic oils also do not offer any physical benefits. Training your eyes and nose to appreciate naturally produced soaps takes a while, but I have grown to appreciate and prefer the subtle palette of colours that can only be achieved through bio-sources, and have found it challenging and beneficial to create pleasurable aromas using only essential oils.

Supplements

These are referred to in soap-making as nutrients, botanicals, secondary ingredients or additions. Supplemental ingredients (usually of edible or floral origin) are additions that are not necessary for saponification. They are classed separately from materials used for colouring or scenting, although many supplements contribute to the colour and, to a lesser extent, the scent of the soap. In general, a supplement is any ingredient that adds texture (oatmeal, cornmeal), adds to the presentation (flowers, shells) or increases the physical therapeutic value of the soap (aloe vera juice, vitamin E oil).

You can use almost any safe natural resource to add physical qualities to your soap. Supplements, such as coffee grounds, are active on different levels, contributing to the colour, texture and scent of the soap. And most essential oils, although classified specifically as scent, also have therapeutic benefits.

opposite 1 Various essential oils and exotic supplemental oils **2** Honey **3** Dried goat's milk **4** Poppy seeds **5** Beeswax **6** Scotch oats **7** Cornmeal **8** Star anise **9** Lavender buds **10** Orange peel **11** Cloves **12** Marigolds **13** Rose buds **14** Blue mallow **15** Cucumber and carrot

left Bentonite Clay & Tea Tree Oil Soap promotes healthy skin.

moulds & other equipment

When making hand-made soap, any plastic or cardboard container can be used as a mould. Cardboard containers will have to be lined first. Care must be taken to insulate small moulds thoroughly because lost heat can cause the oils to separate. This means that the soap will take longer to harden or even be ruined completely. Wood can be used safely but does not make a good mould. It is porous, causing the soap to stick, and inflexible, making the soap difficult to demould. It is also quickly worn down by the caustic soap. Ceramic and glass can be used, but are similarly problematic. Never use aluminium moulds with raw soap. Even stainless steel, which can be used as a mixing pot, is not recommended for moulding. Metal can be used for moulding cured soaps (in milling) or for speciality shapes made with biscuit (cookie) cutters.

In terms of equipment, you will need a sink for clearing up spills and to act as a hot or cold water bath. You will also need a selection of glass, plastic or stainless steel equipment such as spoons and bowls. Aluminium equipment will be corroded by the lye solution and will also contaminate the soap.

Caustic soda (lye) and essential oils must be measured precisely, so get a good electronic scale that measures small amounts accurately (in 5g/⅛oz increments or smaller). The base oils are heavy, so the scales will also need to go up to about 3kg (6lb 9oz). If you can't find a scale

left A selection of moulds including plastic containers, bowls, ice-cube trays, cups, cardboard boxes, pastry cutters and fruit tartlet cases.

that does both, use two different ones. Having several different plastic or glass measuring cups means you don't need to wash up each time you measure. Use a jug (pitcher) for weighing liquid oils and measuring water, and a bowl for weighing caustic soda and mixing supplements.

above **1** Double boiler **2** Large plastic mixing bucket and plastic measuring and pouring jugs (pitchers) **3** Large stainless steel "soap-making pan" **4** Grater **5** Greaseproof (waxed) paper **6** Thick towels **7** Cardboard **8** Pair of scissors **9** Heavy rubber spatulas **10** Large stainless steel mixing spoon **11** Small wooden mixing spoon **12** Large sharp knife **13** Small stainless steel mixing spoon **14** Ladle **15** Pair of thermometers **16** A paintbrush **17** Solid oil for greasing mould **18** Stove **19** Electric scales

1 Apron **2** Rubber gloves **3** Thin latex gloves **4** White vinegar **5** Safety goggles

safety

As long as you learn a few simple rules, use common sense and most of all take care, soap-making is a safe hobby. Sodium hydroxide and newly saponified soap are highly caustic. Soap should be left to cure for a minimum of four weeks before it is used and will become milder with age. (I find that after three months soap will have cured to its optimum mildness and hardness.)

1 Always wear safety goggles, from the beginning to the end of the soap-making process and when cleaning up. The kind that fit flush to the face are best. They are inexpensive and available at DIY (hardware) and paint shops.

2 Wear heavy-duty rubber gloves, especially when cleaning up. Thinner latex gloves can be worn where you need a bit more control, but they will get damaged easily and do not protect the wrists.

3 Keep curious children and pets out of the house or make the soap away from them. As children tend to want to be involved in adult projects and animals cannot logically understand that what you are doing could harm them, I would not feel safe having either around during saponification or curing.

4 Keep a set of soap-making utensils, wash them after use, and store them away from the kitchen.

5 Wear a protective apron, and clothes and shoes that you don't mind receiving burn marks.

6 Keep a bottle of white vinegar nearby in order to neutralize any caustic spillage on your skin.

7 Caustic soda (lye) is poisonous. If ingested, drink water and contact a poison control centre. If it splashes you in the eyes, rinse with clear water for at least half an hour and then get to a casualty department. Fumes are released when caustic soda is mixed with water, so avert your head or leave the room.

8 Always test soap with pH paper before using. It will test between 7.5 and 8.5, which is mild. (A pH reading of 5.5–10 is safe for skin cleanser.)

making soap

Greasing and Lining a Mould

Grease a mould using a paintbrush dipped into melted fat. If you grease the mould well enough you may find that lining is unnecessary.

For a wooden, cardboard or large primary mould that will contain an entire batch or a double batch of soap, greasing and lining is best.

2 Roughly cut two pieces of greaseproof (waxed) paper so that they are long enough to fit the base and sides of the mould. Try the paper for size first.

4 Grease the first piece of paper with the melted oil and "glue" the second piece of paper on top. Smooth down the base and sides.

1 Grease the mould well, using a paintbrush dipped in solid fat melted on the cooker.

3 Fold in the edges of both pieces of paper to fit the mould. Smooth the first piece of paper across the base and up the sides.

5 Trim the paper lining close to the top of the mould or turn the paper over the sides of the mould and tape down.

Using Special Moulds

Using small or special moulds is not easy, so perfect making a basic batch of soap first. Speciality moulds work best with milled or extra-hard soap.

Tips on Special Moulds

• Don't try to demould the soap too soon as this can lead to deforming and cracking.

• Cold-process soap that is still very soft and creamy-looking after a few days may take days or even weeks to set.

• Cold-process soap that has separated in the moulds is not normally usable. After a week, pour off the excess oil, demould and pH test to be sure.

• The freezer method (see step 4) allows you to demould soaps easily and more quickly, but if it has not hardened sufficiently, the final soap will be deformed.

1 Choose appropriate moulds and grease well.

2 Pour or spoon your soap mixture into the moulds.

3 Insulate the soap only if you need to. Remember that insulation is necessary when using small moulds with raw soap. Use three towels or blankets and stack upwards to conserve heat. Insulation is not necessary for soap that has been milled.

4 Leave the soap to harden for three days or longer. Tap the mould to release the soap once it has started to pull away from the mould. If you can't remove the soap or wait another day, freeze for three hours or over-night and dunk into hot water before turning out on to paper.

Basic Soap Base

To make hand-cut bars of basic soap or hand-milled soaps, the first part of the soap-making process is the same. You will need to make a batch of basic soap by mixing the melted fats and/or oils with the lye water, pouring into a mould, and leaving to cure.

615g/1lb 5½oz coconut oil (solid)
670g/1lb 7¾oz sunflower oil
670g/1lb 7¾oz olive oil
295g/10¾oz caustic soda (lye)
930ml/32¼fl oz still mineral water

2 Melt the solid oil first.

3 Add the liquid oils to the pan and then remove from the heat.

5 Pour the water into a large plastic bucket and add the caustic soda to the water, not the other way around, to make lye water. Begin stirring as soon as you start adding the caustic soda to prevent it solidifying into a slick mass like ice on the base of the bucket. This causes problems with the finished soap.

1 These are the ingredients you will need for the Basic Soap Base.

4 Weigh the caustic soda into thin plastic bags.

6 The oils and lye water should be 35–36.7°C/95–98°F.

7 Add the lye water to the oils.

8 Stir continuously until the soap traces. The mixture will thicken after a while, slowly becoming more opaque. Tracing occurs when the mixture thickens further and the impression of a line of soap can be seen on the surface after drizzling from a spatula. Tracing can occur in minutes or take over a day – 40 minutes is the usual time.

9 Add colours and supplements, then the scent, while stirring.

10 Pour into a prepared mould.

11 Cover with cardboard and thick towels. Set for 24 hours.

12 To demould, wear gloves and goggles – the soap is still caustic at this point. Turn the mould upside down on to greaseproof (waxed) paper and press from the back. Remove the lining paper.

13 Cut the soap into bars within 24–36 hours of setting to stop it getting too hard. Leave to cure in a warm dry place on greaseproof (waxed) paper.

Tips on the Basic Soap Base

• Use a light-coloured olive oil. Virgin or extra virgin oils produce soft soaps and add time to the saponification process.

• Keep caustic soda (lye) covered until it is weighed. Exposed to the air, it attracts water molecules, which add to the weight and decrease the strength of the lye.

• Water and oil measurements should be more or less accurate in a recipe. A little variation will not greatly affect the outcome of a batch of soap. Caustic soda, however, must be measured with the utmost accuracy, to avoid unexpected results.

• Bringing the liquids to the correct temperature takes practice. If you have problems synchronizing them, fill the sink with hot or cold water to warm or cool the liquids quickly. Warm up oil that has cooled too much for a few seconds on the stove.

• A wide rubber spatula is the best tool to blend the soap mixture, to mix in supplements and to remove all the soap from the pot, but you can continue to use a stainless steel spoon.

• Tracing is affected by many factors, including temperature (it is best to make soap in a warmish room) and different ingredients. If soap takes longer than an hour to trace, leave it and stir occasionally until it thickens. As long as measurements were accurate and you used pure, unexposed caustic soda (lye), then it should trace.

Some batches of soap, such as those containing lots of olive oil or set at too low or high a temperature, can even take all night to trace. If you can see a thin layer of separated oil in the pan, don't pour the soap. Leave in a warm place and continue mixing until the soap is completely homogenized.

• Putting the supplement in soon after tracing will allow more of the colour of the botanical to be released than if it is put in just before pouring when the mixture is thicker.

• Some essential oils can greatly slow down or speed up the saponification process. Learn to avoid or use this to your advantage.

• Allow the soap to cure for at least one month before using.

• Test the pH of your first few batches of soap with pH paper to ensure mildness. A reading of 8–8.5 is most normal, and anywhere between 5.5–10 is completely safe.

Moisturizing Soap Base

This is a mild, moisturizing soap with good lathering qualities. To make, follow the steps for the Basic Soap Base, but use the ingredients listed below. You can make other moisturizing soaps by adding different supplements to this recipe.

610g/1lb 5½oz coconut oil
670g/1lb 7¾oz sunflower oil
670g/1lb 7¾oz olive oil
240g/8½oz caustic soda (lye)
930ml/32¾fl oz still mineral water

Castile Block Base

This is a traditional style of soap that originated in Spain and the Mediterranean. It usually contains a large quantity of, if not only, olive oil. As pure olive oil soap made from good-grade oil can take up to a day to saponify, I have devised a recipe that preserves the benefits and traditional appeal of olive oil, while avoiding the problems of an excessively long trace time or a soft sticky soap. This Castile-style recipe produces extremely hard, sturdy bars that stand up

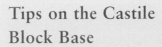

Tips on the Castile Block Base

• Cut into large, sturdy chunks and use in the shower or kitchen as an all-purpose soap.
• Adding beeswax speeds up the trace time, so have your moulds ready.

well to water. To make this soap, follow the instructions for the Basic Soap Base, but use the ingredients listed below and pour the liquids together at 54.4°C/130°F. You can make a variety of soaps by adding other supplements to this recipe.

150g/5¼oz beeswax
250g/8¾oz palm oil
250g/8¾oz coconut oil
1300g/2lb 12oz olive oil
265g/9½oz caustic soda (lye)
930ml/32¾fl oz still mineral
    water

Hand-milled Soap Base

A batch of basic soap can be grated, remelted and moulded to produce hand-milled soap. Scents, supplements and colours can also be added. The texture of the grated soap will resemble anything between grated Cheddar and powdery Parmesan, depending on the consistency of the original soap. The smaller the slivers of grated soap, the better the finished soap will be. Remember that if you are rebatching a failed soap, which already has added ingredients, you may not want to add further ingredients.

800g/1¼lb grated soap

320ml/11¼fl oz mineral water

25g/1oz any essential oil

colours, scents and supplements

   (optional)

1 Grate the set soap into a plastic bowl. Its appearance will depend on the original soap.

2 The amount of water that you will need to mix with the gratings will affect the hardness and drying time of the finished soap. Start by adding about 100ml/3½fl oz of water to a double boiler and allow to heat through.

3 Add the soap gratings and bring to a simmer. Fold the mixture slowly until the soap is glossy and resembles melted cheese. Only add more water little by little if the gratings appear dry and crumbly. Do not whip or whisk, as this incorporates excessive air.

4 Mix in the colours, scents, oil and supplements, if necessary.

5 Pour or spoon the mixture into your prepared moulds.

6 Allow the soap to dry. It is not necessary to insulate soap that you have hand-milled, but you will have to leave the soap to dry for at least three days in a dry place before removing from the moulds. Before using, dry for at least a further three weeks to harden the soap.

Tips on the Hand-milled Soap Base

• The consistency as well as the moisture content of hand-milled soap will vary depending on the original soap that you decide to use. As a general rule, however, I would advise that the volume of water you can add should be up to, but not over, 40 per cent of the weight of the soap – that is, you may safely add up to 400ml/ 14fl oz of liquid to 1kg/2¼lb of the grated soap

• If you are planning to add other liquid supplements, such as honey or aloe vera juice, to hand-milled soap, then you will need to take this into account when working out the total amount of liquid in the soap, and reduce the amount of water you add accordingly.

• Adding 25g/1oz of essential oil is generally suitable for 800g/1¾lb of soap (about three per cent). In general, you can successfully add up to five per cent of the total weight of all the ingredients used in order to create a soap with a powerful aroma.

• The quantities of supplements and colours used are a matter of personal choice, but, as a general guide, I suggest adding no more than 30 per cent of the weight of soap used and no more than five per cent if the supplement you have chosen is an oil.

• Use a rubber spatula to stir the soap mixture.

• Milled soaps demould more easily from speciality moulds and hold their shape much better when they have been left in the moulds for a week or more, rather than three days.

problem solving

Soap seems normal but breaks or cracks on demoulding
Soap has been demoulded too quickly or the mould has been manipulated too much. Roll into balls or save for milling.

Soap cracks easily or is waxy and crumbly, although pH is fine
Soap has been poured at too low a temperature or has lost heat too rapidly while setting. This is an aesthetic problem. Make soap in a warm room and insulate well.

Dry, brittle soap or large amounts of white powder on top
This is caused by too much caustic soda (lye). Leave for six weeks, then pH test to see if it is too alkaline (above pH 10). If it is, discard the batch and do not attempt to mill.

Thick layer of separated oil on top of soap after setting
The soap will probably be too caustic because too much oil separated out. This is due to too low a pouring temperature or rapid temperature loss, or – most commonly – insufficient stirring. Make sure the soap traces and that there is no oil floating on top of the mixture before pouring.

left Cinnamon & Orange Soap.

No tracing or thickening
This problem usually occurs when soap has been poured at too low a temperature, left to cool without stirring, or contains insufficient or contaminated caustic soda (lye).

If you can discount these reasons, continue stirring the mixture since the trace time is also affected by the choice of ingredients. For example, if you are using only or mostly virgin olive oil and certain essential oils, saponification could be slowed down. If you have used insufficient caustic soda (lye) or there is a temperature-related problem, continue stirring the mixture for as long as you can manage and pour anyway. However, the resulting soap may be poor quality.

Soap contains air pockets filled with liquid

This is due to insufficient stirring or rapid setting, sometimes caused by certain essential oils or supplements. The soap cannot be used as it is, but can usually be milled successfully.

Soft and oily powdery soap

This is usually due to setting at too low or high a temperature. The soap may be mild enough, but save any that is excessively powdery for milling.

Soft toffee-like soap

This is due to insufficient or poor quality caustic soda. Cure for an extra three to five weeks. Soap like this can be too fatty for cleansing, but is not harmful. You can mill it successfully, however, if you mix it with a greater quantity of standard soap.

Thin white film of powder appears on top of soap

Although this film is normal and harmless, scrape, brush or wash it away. To avoid the powder forming, cover the soaps straight after pouring.

Curdling and seizing

If very opaque, curd-like masses form in what seems to be an otherwise fine batch of soap, it is usually due to certain essential oils like clove. If the soap isn't hardening too quickly, strain through a pair of tights stretched over a bucket. If the soap begins to seize, quickly pour into a mould before it sets solid in the pan. Curdling and seizing like this will not affect the quality of the soap. (Very high temperatures can also cause curdling, resulting in undesirable or unusable soap.)

above Rope Soap makes an amusing gift.

Thin layer of separated oil on top of soap after setting

This is a minor problem that can occur because of insufficient stirring, a temperature drop or when making a moisturizing soap. Leave the soap to harden for a few extra days to see if the oil will "soak in". Otherwise, wipe off the excess oil and allow the soap to cure as usual. The soap will usually be fine, but pH test if you are not certain.

goat's milk & almond soap

How to make

Basic Soap Base

Follow the instructions for making the Basic Soap Base on pages 26–27, but use the supplements and essential oils listed below.

Supplements

200g/7oz dried goat's milk
200g/7oz almond butter (a nut butter available from most health food shops)
100ml/3$\frac{1}{2}$fl oz almond oil

Essential Oils

15g/$\frac{1}{2}$oz cedar oil
30g/1$\frac{1}{4}$oz lavender oil
20g/$\frac{3}{4}$oz petitgrain oil
1 tsp sweet orange oil

Goat's milk produces a protein-rich and conditioning soap, while almond oil is a good moisturizer. The essential oils used here will nourish both the skin and the spirit. Although you can obtain fresh goat's milk from large supermarkets, I prefer to use a dried version, which is available from health food shops or through your chemist (drugstore). The dried milk will not affect moisture content, and you will achieve a higher concentration of milk protein than with liquid milk.

1 Add the powdered goat's milk and the almond butter to the almond oil. Mix thoroughly until the ingredients form a paste. Add this paste with the essential oils to the Basic Soap Base at step 9.

honey & oatmeal soap

How to make

Basic Soap Base

Follow the instructions for making the Basic Soap Base on pages 26–27, but use the supplements and essential oil listed below.

Supplements

300g/11oz rolled oats

350g/12oz runny honey

Essential Oil

80g/3¼oz benzoin oil

This is a soap that makes me think of home-made cookies because of the warm, delicate, vanilla-like scent of the benzoin and, of course, the quantity of oats and honey included. Besides encouraging your appetite with its homely smell, this soap will also promote healthy skin. Oats are good for exfoliating the skin, and are beneficial for skin conditions such as eczema, cold sores and shingles, while honey is healing, nutritive and moisturizing.

1 Mix the honey and benzoin oil together with the oats in a plastic jug (pitcher). Add this mixture to the basic soap base before pouring into your prepared mould.

clove soap

How to make

Basic Soap Base

Follow the instructions for making the Basic Soap Base on pages 26–27, but use the supplement and essential oil listed below.

Supplement

clove buds, to decorate

Essential Oil

60g/2¼oz clove oil

Tips

- Cut the soap into fat, randomly sized blocks to add to its rustic appeal.
- Clove oil accelerates the trace time and setting of the soap, so drizzle in the oil very carefully, while stirring steadily – as if you were making mayonnaise.

Studded with cloves and delicately scented with clove essential oil, this soap would make a lovely autumn or winter gift. As the winter nights draw in, there is nothing quite like a bath filled with the pungent, spicy scent of cloves to uplift your spirits and to revive you if you are feeling tired. Therapeutically, cloves are stimulating and carminative; the buds and oil are also used to treat nausea and migraine.

1 Cut the finished soap into large, randomly sized chunks and push the clove buds into the top of each piece. Try to keep the layer of cloves as even as possible for an attractive finish.

rose heart soaps

How to make

Basic Soap Base

Follow the instructions for making the Basic Soap Base on pages 26–27, but use the supplement and essential oils listed below.

Supplement

25g/1oz rose petals

Essential Oils

40g/1$^1/_2$oz rose otto or geranium oil

10g/$^1/_4$oz lavender oil

1 tsp petitgrain oil

1 tsp vetivert oil

Tips

- Use the left-overs from cutting out the rose heart shapes to make soap balls.

There is something about hearts and roses that makes people smile – we associate both with the joys of romance. I am not particularly fond of floral scents, but I love this soap. It has a well-balanced aroma, and the abundance of rose buds is charming and sweetly decadent. Rose has the added advantage of relieving depression, as well as acting as an aphrodisiac and a sedative. Applied to the skin, rose has healing and rejuvenating qualities.

1 Cut out the heart shapes on a smooth surface using a cookie cutter, applying pressure evenly. Use rose buds to decorate the top of each soap and finish off by sprinkling with rose petals.

cinnamon seed soap

How to make

Basic Soap Base

Follow the instructions for
making the Basic Soap Base
on pages 26–27, but use
the colours, supplements
and essential oil
listed below.

Colours

70g/2³/₄oz powdered instant
tea or coffee

Supplements

110g/4¹/₄oz seed mixture
(such as poppy, caraway and
psylium seeds)

Essential Oil

60g/2¹/₄oz cinnamon leaf oil

This beautifully scented soap has exfoliating properties and is very satisfying to use as a massage bar. The small seeds will eventually wash away as the soap is used and go safely down the drain.

1 After mixing in the seeds and oil, put 500–700ml (16–22 fl oz) of the traced soap into a separate jug and add the tea.

3 Use the end of a spoon or knife to make a winding, snake-like pattern from the top of the mould to the bottom.

2 Slowly pour the tea mixture into the large mould containing the uncoloured soap to create an irregular pattern.

4 Repeat the pattern, starting from one side of the mould and moving across to the other. Allow to set and cure as usual.

flower cupcake soaps

How to make

Hand-milled Soap Base

Follow the instructions for
making the Hand-milled
Soap Base on pages 30–31,
but use the colour,
supplements and essential
oils listed below.

Colour

10–15g/$^1/_4$–$^1/_2$oz ground
turmeric

Supplements

dried yellow and burgundy
peony flowers or other
large blooms

Essential Oils

20g/$^3/_4$oz jasmine oil
10g/$^1/_4$oz ylang-ylang oil
1 tsp grapefruit oil

This is a whimsical soap that is ideally made in the spring when
garden flowers are starting to come into their own. I imagine
these soaps being given as favours at a garden party or even at
an older child's birthday. Jasmine oil is an expensive oil, so
making a milled soap, which uses smaller quantities, is more
affordable. Bear in mind that these soaps look edible, so ensure
that everyone knows that they are not real cakes. It is best not to
make this soap at home if you have small children.

1 After the soaps have dried and hardened sufficiently in their paper
cases, press the stems of the dried flower buds in to the
surface. Scatter the collection of soaps with any remaining petals.

seaweed soap

How to make

Hand-milled Soap Base

Follow the instructions for making the Hand-milled Soap Base on pages 30–31, but use the colours, supplements and essential oils listed below.

Colours

50g/2oz powdered green-blue algae or chlorophyll

Supplements

70g/2³/₄oz bladderwrack
50g/2oz Iceland moss
the juice of one lemon

Essential Oils

15g/¹/₂oz bergamot oil
20g/³/₄oz patchouli oil
1 tsp lime oil

Tips

- The soaking water contains valuable minerals.

Seaweed retains moisture and contains an abundance of beneficial minerals, including iodine. It is used cosmetically to reduce impurities in fat cells and to nourish and improve the skin. Bladderwrack is taken internally as a metabolic stimulant and used topically to ease rheumatic conditions. Many people do not like the smell of seaweed, but the bergamot and lime oils will help to counteract the odour. Make this soap for yourself or for a dedicated spa goer.

1 Soak the seaweed in the juice of a lemon mixed with a little warm water for about 30 minutes. Drain, and use the soaking water to replace the quantity of water specified in the Hand-milled Soap Base.

frankincense & myrrh soap

Moisturizing Soap Base

Follow the instructions for making the Moisturizing Soap Base on page 29, but use the colour, supplements and essential oils listed below.

Colour

80g/3¹/₄oz mixed herbs

Supplements

silver and gold leaf, to decorate

Essential Oils

30g/1¹/₄oz frankincense oil
40g/1¹/₂oz myrrh oil

Tips

- For specific designs, use the gold and silver leaf that comes mounted on paper and cut into the shape you require before applying.

Frankincense and myrrh are resinous gums that have been used since antiquity for their spiritual and physical benefits. They are used in one form or another by many cultures, often as a perfume, and appear in the Old and New Testaments. Therapeutically, frankincense slows down and deepens breathing, is useful for many pulmonary ailments and is said to delay the appearance of wrinkles. Myrrh is antifungal, healing and anti-inflammatory.

1 After the soap has set and been cut into blocks, use silver or gold leaf to decorate the top. To create a random pattern, apply the leaf a little at a time rather than laying a single sheet at once.

cinnamon & orange soap

How to make

Basic Soap Base

Follow the instructions for making the Basic Soap Base on pages 26–27, but use the supplements and essential oils listed below.

Supplements

80g/3¹/₄oz diced orange peel slices of whole orange, to decorate

Essential Oils

20g/³/₄oz cinnamon leaf oil
65g/2¹/₂oz sweet orange oil

Tips

- Be careful not to stack the curing soap because this will spoil the orange segments.
- Grapefruit seed extract acts as a natural preservative. After the soap has set, paint the surface with a mixture of 8–10 drops of this extract in vegetable oil.

Although cinnamon and orange are traditionally associated with Christmas, this soap makes a perfect present at any time. Cinnamon is stimulating and warming, while orange is a cooling sedative. Extracts from both plants are used internally for their carminative qualities. Citrus oil extends the saponification process, while cinnamon reduces it, so that the resulting soap sets completely and evenly in a reasonable amount of time, without seizing or curdling.

1 Place the orange segments on top of the newly poured soap. Ensure that the slices remain floating on the surface of the soap. After the soap has set, paint with the grapefruit extract mixture (see Tips).

lavender olive oil soap

How to make

Castile Block Base

Follow the instructions for making the Castile Block Base on page 29, but use the supplements and essential oil listed below.

Supplements

lavender buds, to decorate

Essential Oil

70g/2³/₄oz lavender oil

Tips

- Lavender is a herb with many health benefits. For example, lavender soap can be used to ease the irritation of chafed skin.
- Keep soap that is not yet being used in the linen cupboard to scent sheets and pillow cases.

Most people adore the scent of lavender, as it can evoke a sense of times gone by, when lavender was used to scent rooms, cupboards and wardrobes in sachets and pomanders. Lavender-scented soap comes from the same line of traditional toiletries. This Castile-style soap, which combines both traditional ingredients and fragrance, is particularly attractive, the delicate white of the soap contrasting with the lavender-blue of the flower buds. The olive oil also has moisturizing properties.

1 When the soap is ready, cut into fairly large, randomly sized slices and decorate by pressing the top of each piece into a shallow tray of lavender buds.

soap balls

How to make

Moisturizing Soap Base

Follow the instructions for
making the Moisturizing Soap
Base on page 29, but use the
colours, supplements and
essential oils listed below.
You will need 100g/4oz
grated Moisturizing Soap
Base for each soap ball.

red rose petals, orange
flowers, lavender buds,
mixed herbs, cinnamon bark
pieces and cinnamon powder

You will need $1/2$ tsp
essential oil per ball. Choose
from the following oils:
rose or rose geranium oil
neroli or mandarin oil
lavender oil
sage oil
cinnamon leaf oil

This is one of my favourite ways to remould or recycle soap. Soap balls
are adorable, and you can make a few or a whole batch of them in a number
of different varieties. They are also easy and relatively quick to make.

1 Add the essential oil you have chosen
for the particular batch to the grated
soap and mix together.

2 Weigh and roll together 100g/4oz for
each ball, until they are compact and
without air bubbles. Add oil or water if dry.

3 Coat each ball in the appropriate
flower or herb (the one that matches
the essential oil used; mixed herbs would
complement the sage oil, for example). If
the herbs or flowers do not stick, moisten
the surface of each ball by rolling it
between palms moistened with water.

rope soap

How to make

Moisturizing Soap Base

Follow the instructions for making the Moisturizing Soap Base on page 29, but use the supplements and essential oils listed below. You will need 325g/11½oz grated Moisturizing Soap Base for each soap ball.

Supplements

40g/1½oz chopped orange peel and 30g/1¼oz poppy seeds per soap

Essential Oils

15g/½oz bay or lime oil per soap

This soap is great fun to make – everyone remembers giving these chunky soaps on the end of a piece of rope to their father or grandfather. These soaps are beautifully scented with bay or lime oil.

1 Make a slip knot at one end of the rope to form a "hanger" for the soap. Tie the other end into a simple knot.

2 Stick the grated soap around the rope close to the end with the simple knot; use 325g/11½oz grated soap per ball.

3 Continue to press the grated soap around the rope until you achieve a tight, even ball. A final decorative touch, especially if you want to give the soap as a gift, is to press a shell into the surface of the soap ball. You could also present the soap in a gift box.

vanilla neapolitan bars

How to make

Hand-milled Soap Base

Follow the instructions for making the Hand-milled Soap Base on pages 30–31, but use the colours and essential oils listed below. You will need to make the mould shown here to create the distinctive shape.

Colours

First layer: 20ml/4 tsp raw beetroot (beet) juice

Third layer: 100g/4oz plain (semi-sweet) chocolate

Essential Oils

First layer: 20g/³/₄oz benzoin oil

Third layer: 70g/2³/₄oz benzoin oil

Tips

- Treat each layer as a separate soap and allow to dry before pouring in the next layer.
- Dry the final soap for three to four weeks before using.

This soap takes time to achieve, but the result is well worth the effort. It is scented with benzoin, which is less expensive than vanilla absolute. The dark layer contains chocolate which contributes to the soap's rich colour.

1 Using a lidded box, cut off one side of both the box and the lid.

3 Tape the lid and box together to form an upright, leak-proof mould.

2 Using a pen and ruler, draw in the three levels to the required depth for each layer of soap.

4 Grease and line the mould. Pour in the first layer to the required level. Allow to dry, then pour in the next layer and so on.

pumice soap

How to make

Basic Soap Base

Follow the instructions for making the Basic Soap Base on pages 26–27, but use the colours and supplement listed below, adding them at step 9.

Colours

200g/7oz fine oatmeal

165g/5$\frac{1}{2}$oz finely ground coffee

65g/2$\frac{1}{2}$oz ground pumice

Supplement

20g/$\frac{3}{4}$oz grapefruit seed extract

Tips

- This soap is too abrasive for the face or body. It should only be used on the hands and feet.
- Be vigilant, as grapefruit seed extract speeds up the trace time.
- If you can't find powdered pumice, wrap a piece of pumice in several layers of thick plastic and hit with a hammer.

This is a real working person's hand cleanser. Pumice, oats and coffee are all abrasives that will smooth away rough, calloused skin and scrub off grime such as engine oil and paint that has soaked into the skin. Additionally, grapefruit seed extract kills germs. Coffee also has the added benefit of absorbing odours. Make this soap for someone whose hands or feet need extra attention and care. It should not be used on delicate skin.

bentonite clay & tea tree oil soap

This soap is helpful for infected or oily acne-prone skin. Famously from Australia, tea tree oil is distilled from the tree of the same name. It can be used internally and externally for a variety of complaints. It is a broad-spectrum antibiotic and antifungal that promotes immune response, making it popular among backpackers and people on holiday. Bentonite clay is a cosmetic-grade clay that is mildly abrasive and absorbs oil.

How to make

Basic Soap Base

Follow the instructions for making the Basic Soap Base on pages 26–27, but use the colour, supplement and essential oil listed below, adding them at step 9.

Colour

30g/1¼oz paprika

Supplement

200g/7oz bentonite clay

Essential Oil

50g/2oz tea tree oil

glossary

Antibacterial/antifungal describes a substance that destroys harmful pathogens like bacteria or fungus.

Bentonite clay a mildly abrasive cosmetic-grade clay in a variety of colours that absorbs oil.

Carminative relieves flatulence and digestive discomfort.

Cold process the process described in this book in which soap is made using only the heat from the chemical reaction of the forming soap.

Cured soap soap that has rested long enough to reach a pH value that is safe to use on the skin.

Essential oil the substance in a plant that is responsible for its odour. The oil comes from various parts of the plant and is removed by distillation, expulsion or through solvent extraction.

Lye a common term for sodium hydroxide or caustic soda.

Milling grating and melting down a set soap to make a new soap.

Petitgrain oil an essential oil extracted from unripe orange fruits. Sweet orange and neroli essential oils are also extracted from the same plant.

pH the acidic or alkaline nature of a substance. (A reading of 5.5 is the natural pH of the skin, making it slightly acidic; 7 is a neutral pH; 8 is the average pH of mild soap, making it slightly alkaline.)

pH paper a specially coated paper that indicates pH.

Primary mould a large mould for an entire batch of soap or a basic mould to set soap to be milled or specially shaped.

Raw soap describes caustic soap that has not reached a mild state and newly set soap.

Rebatching recycling a cured soap into a new soap or toiletry.

Saponification the chemical combining and homogenization of oil with an alkaline solution (the lye water).

Seizing the rapid and almost instant solidifying of newly mixed soap which makes it difficult or impossible to pour. This is usually due to the addition of certain essential oils and supplements or a temperature problem.

Sodium hydroxide the chemical name for caustic soda.

Trace the pattern that is visible on the surface of a quantity of soap when it has begun to saponify, and a small amount is drizzled back into the soap.

suppliers

UNITED KINGDOM

Essential and Speciality Oils
Meadows of Canterbury
Unit 2
Stour Valley Business Park
Canterbury
Kent CT4 7HS
Tel: 01227 731489

Dried Herbs and Botanicals
Neal's Yard Remedies
68 Chalk Farm Road
London NW1 8AN
Tel: 0171 284 2039

Hambledon Herbs
Court Farm
Milverton
Somerset TA4 INF
Tel: 01823 401205

Bulk Oils
Lake Food Euro Ltd.
26–100 Scrubs Lane
London NW10 6RE
Tel: 0181 968 0261

Pride Oil Products Ltd.
Pride House
Unit 2
South Way
Wembley HA9
Tel: 0181 900 0439

UNITED STATES

Angel's Earth
1633 Scheffer Avenue
St. Paul, MN 55116
Tel: (612) 698-3601
Fax: (612) 698-3636
a-earth@concentric.net

Creation Herbal Products
P.O. Box 344
10492 U.S. Highway 421
Deep Gap, NC 28618
www.creationherbal.com

Sweet Cakes
Soapmaking Supplies
249 North Road
Kinnelon, NJ 07405
Tel: (973) 492-7406
www.sweetcakes.com

AUSTRALIA

Australian Botanical Products
39 Malverton Drive
Hallam VIC 3803
Ph: 03 9796 4833
Fax: 03 9796 4966
Email: usbot@ozemail.com.au

The Bach Flower Shop
349 Little Collins St
Melbourne 3000 VIC
Ph: (03) 9670 5933

AMCAL
Unit 2, 50-52 Redfern
Wetherall Park NSW 2164
Ph: 9757 2508
Fax: 9757 3463

index

author's acknowledgements

I imagined a company full of feeling, purpose and integrity. I could not have realized this dream completely on my own. Thank you to Elisabeth, Anna, Caroline, Jessica and Rebecca and Abdu, Annika, Anthony, Aranzazu, Beth, Henrik, Kasper, Kristina, Merethe, Patricia, Salvatore, Suzannah and Vikki who all help to keep Savonnerie so amazing. A special thank you to Reg Valin and Darryn at Meadows, Paul at MJS, and Rob Mays, who have always been so helpful and supportive from the beginning.